Living in MOUNTAINS

Tea Benduhn

Reading consultant: Susan Nations, M.Ed., author/literacy coach/
consultant in literacy development

WEEKLY READER®
PUBLISHING

Please visit our web site at: www.garethstevens.com
For a free color catalog describing our list of high-quality books,
call 1-800-542-2595 (USA) or 1-800-387-3178 (Canada).

Library of Congress Cataloging-in-Publication Data

Benduhn, Tea.
   Living in mountains / Tea Benduhn.
      p. cm. — (Life on the edge)
   ISBN-10: 0-8368-8342-X (lib. bdg.)
   ISBN-13: 978-0-8368-8342-8 (lib. bdg.)
   ISBN-10: 0-8368-8347-0 (softcover)
   ISBN-13: 978-0-8368-8347-3 (softcover)
      1. Mountains—Juvenile literature.   2. Human geography—
Juvenile literature.   I. Title.
   GF57.B46   2008
   910.914'3—dc22   2007014709

This edition first published in 2008 by
Weekly Reader® Books
An imprint of Gareth Stevens Publishing
1 Reader's Digest Road
Pleasantville, NY 10570-7000 USA

Copyright © 2008 by Gareth Stevens, Inc.

Managing editor: Mark Sachner
Art direction: Tammy West
Picture research: Sabrina Crewe
Production: Jessica Yanke

Picture credits: cover, title page Bobby Model/National Geographic/Getty Images; p. 5 Michael Darter/
Photonica/Getty Images; p. 6 Scott Krall/© Gareth Stevens, Inc.; p. 7 James Hager/Robert Harding World
Imagery/Getty Images; p. 9 NASA; p. 10 David Noton/The Image Bank/Getty Images; p. 11 © Dallas and
John Heaton/Free Agents Limited/Corbis; p. 13 Louis Psihoyos/Science Faction/Getty Images; p. 14
© Mark A. Johnson/Corbis; p. 15 © Anneliese Villiger/Zefa/Corbis; p. 16 Fati Moalusi/AFP/Getty Images;
p. 17 © Bo Zaunders/Corbis; p. 19 © George Steinmetz/Corbis; p. 20 © Karl Maret/Corbis; Terry Donnelly/
Stone/Getty Images.

Printed in the United States of America

1 2 3 4 5 6 7 8 9 11 10 09 08 07

MCk

DATE DUE

TABLE OF CONTENTS

Cover and title page: Steep mountain slopes are fun to ski down!

CHAPTER *1*

Welcome to the Mountains

The air is crisp and fresh. You take deep breaths to get enough **oxygen**. Cold winds blow very fast. The land is so steep it looks like a wall of rocks ahead of you. Behind you, a sharp cliff drops more than 1,000 feet (305 meters). If you make one wrong move, you might fall to your death. Where are you? You are in the mountains!

The mountains are **extreme** places to live. No other land on Earth is as high as the mountains. Mount Everest is the world's tallest mountain. It is 29,035 feet (8,850 m) above sea level. That is more than 5 miles (8 kilometers) high!

Mount Everest is dangerous to climb. Many people have died trying. To stay alive, people must climb in teams.

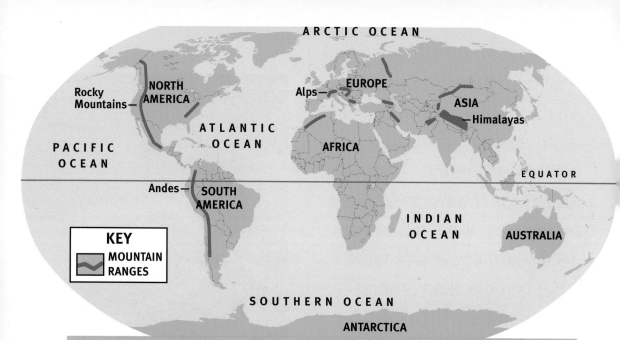

The Rocky Mountains are in North America. The Andes are in South America. The Alps are in Europe. The Himalayas are in Asia. Mount Everest is in the Himalayas.

Mountains are everywhere. They are on every continent. Mountains are even in the ocean! Most mountains are in chains, or groups, called **ranges**. The biggest mountain ranges with the highest mountains are the Rocky Mountains, the Andes, the Alps, and the Himalayas.

The weather and **climate** at the bottom of a mountain are different from the weather and climate at the top. At the bottom, the day can be warm and sunny while the top is covered with snow. As you go up a mountain, the air gets colder. Above the **tree line**, it is too cold for trees to grow. Even higher up, at the **snow line**, the snow never melts.

Many mountains are freezing cold at the top! Trees do not grow above the tree line. Snow does not melt above the snow line.

CHAPTER 2

People of the Mountains

Mountains can be filled with danger. Weather can change quickly from calm to storm. A person can freeze to death or fall hundreds of feet. An **avalanche** or **mudslide** can bury a village. Millions of people, however, feel safe living in the mountains. They find food and shelter in the mountains. These people make the mountains their home.

Mountains are steep and rocky. People have had trouble getting from one side of a mountain to the other. Today, people have many ways of getting around mountains. For thousands of years, however, mountains have kept people apart. They were **borders** between countries. People living on one side of a mountain often had a different way of life than people living on the other side.

The climate is very different on one side of the Rocky Mountains than the other. Many trees and plants grow in California, on the left side of this picture, taken from space. The other side is desert.

Long ago, mountains protected people from attack. They blocked out **invaders** from other lands. All over the world, people have built villages in mountains. They have used trees, mud, and rocks to build their homes. They built walls by stacking huge blocks of stone.

The ancient Incan city Machu Picchu was high in the Andes. For hundreds of years, the mountains hid the city from the outside world.

In Europe, kings built castles high in the mountains to watch over their kingdoms. They could look out for armies that might try to attack them. Today, people from all over the world visit these castles as **tourists**. People living in mountain towns make money that tourists spend.

Many people think castles are beautiful. They come from all over the world to tour castles and buy souvenirs.

CHAPTER 3

Living in the Mountains

Most people who live in mountains grow crops for food. Some foods grow easily on mountains. People grow wheat, rice, corn, fruit, and vegetables. People living in the Andes were the first to discover wild potatoes. More than two hundred types of potatoes grow in mountain areas.

Terraces look like giant steps on the side of a mountain. On the island of Bali, farmers grow crops of rice on mountain terraces.

Farming on mountains is difficult. The sides of mountains are steep slopes. The soil can wear away. To keep crops in place, many farmers make **terraces**. They cut into the sides of mountains to make flat sections. They build stone walls on the edges to hold the land in place.

In Peru, women use hand spindles to spin llama wool into yarn. They use plant dye to make bright colors. They weave cloth to make clothes.

In the mountains, people raise animals, such as cattle, goats, sheep, or llamas. These animals **graze** on mountain grass. They can walk easily on the rocks. In the Andes, people use llamas to carry food and other items for trade. They use llama wool to make clothes.

People make different kinds of music on the mountains. In Switzerland, in the Alps, people **yodel**. They started yodeling as a way to shout to each other across mountaintops. They also used large wooden horns called alpenhorns. Alpenhorns are as long as 13 feet (4 m)!

Alpenhorns make a loud sound that echoes through the mountains.

Ponies are a good way to get around in the mountains of Lesotho.
A wool blanket keeps this man warm in the high, cold air.

For people who live in the mountains, traveling can be difficult. The ground can suddenly become too steep to climb. In other areas, the ground can quickly drop down. People walk on narrow paths or ride animals, such as horses. Lesotho is a small country high in the mountains in Africa. Many people ride ponies to get around the narrow pathways.

People can travel by car or train in the mountains. Roads and train tracks are cut into the sides of mountains and wrap around the edges. Some mountains are too steep for cars or trains to climb. Workers blast holes through the rock to make tunnels. If you ride through the mountains, your ears can hurt, just like on an airplane.

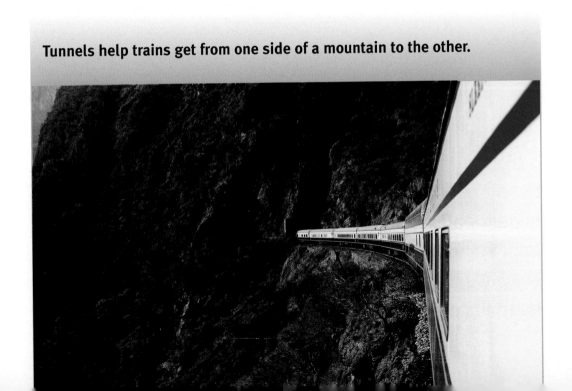

Tunnels help trains get from one side of a mountain to the other.

CHAPTER 4

People and the Mountains Today

People use mountains for their natural **resources**. They mine for metals, such as iron, copper, and gold. They mine for minerals and gems, such as diamonds, too. They also use mountains for **recreation**. Many people go to the mountains to ski or climb.

When people make mines, they damage the land. Some mines are deep holes in the ground. Sometimes, these holes cave in, or **collapse**. In the United States, many people have died in **coal mines**. For other mines, companies remove the top of a mountain. The machines used to dig mines can create a lot of **pollution**.

When people clear areas of mountains to dig mines, other people can lose their homes. Animals can lose their homes, too.

Many people like to vacation in the mountains. People can damage the places they go for fun, however. Some people leave behind lots of trash. The cars and buses they drive create pollution. People can even cause an avalanche if they step in the wrong place.

On some mountains, the number of people allowed to ski is reduced because they can cause avalanches.

Some people want to protect the mountains. Many nations, for example, make some of their mountains into national parks. National parks have rules for the ways people can use them. When people follow the rules, they can help protect the mountains for a very long time.

Rocky Mountain National Park is in Colorado.

Glossary

avalanche – a large mass of snow that falls down a mountainside

climate – the weather and temperature usually found in an area

coal mines – underground pits or tunnels where coal is dug out

collapse – fall in, break apart, or shrink

extreme – more of something, such as height, than we are used to

graze – feed on grass

invaders – those who enter an area to take over or damage it

mudslide – a large amount of mud quickly falling down a slope

oxygen – a gas in the air that we need to breathe in order to live

pollution – human-made waste that harms the environment

ranges – groups of mountains

recreation – activities done to have fun

resources – natural substances that people can use to make their lives better

snow line – the area on a mountain where snow does not melt

terraces – flat areas on the side of a hill on mountains that rise above each other like the steps of a staircase

tourists – people visiting places for recreation

tree line – the area on a mountain above which trees do not grow

yodel – a type of singing that is like shouting

For More Information

Books

Grand Canyon. Rookie Read-About Geography (series). Lisa Trumbauer (Children's Press)

Mountains. Heinemann First Library (series). Angela Royston (Heinemann)

Mountains. Where on Earth? World Geography (series). JoAnn Early Macken (Gareth Stevens)

The Rocky Mountains. Ready-to-Read (series). Marion Dane Bauer (Aladdin Library)

Web Sites

Denali for Kids
pbskids.org/nova/denali/index.html
Click on the links to learn about mountain survival skills.

All About the Great Wall of China
www.enchantedlearning.com/subjects/greatwall
The largest wall in the world is on top of a mountain chain.

Index

About the Author

Tea Benduhn writes and edits books for children and teens. She lives in the beautiful state of Wisconsin with her husband and two cats. The walls of their home are lined with bookshelves filled with books. Tea says, "I read every day. It is more fun than watching television!"